piano/vocal

the jason robert brown collection

D1598016

ISBN 1-4234-0103-4

HAL•LEONARD® CORPORATION

7777 W. BLUEMOUND RD. P.O. BOX 13819 MILWAUKEE, WI 53213

In Australia Contact:
Hal Leonard Australia Pty. Ltd.
4 Lentara Court
Cheltenham, Victoria, 3192 Australia
Email: ausadmin@halleonard.com

Visit Hal Leonard Online at
www.halleonard.com

thoughts from jrb

This folio commemorates the tenth anniversary of my professional debut as a songwriter for the musical theater. It's been an exhilarating, intense and unpredictable ten years, and all the songs in this book are part of that story.

I arrived in New York when I was twenty years old, and I spent my first five years in Manhattan working as a rehearsal pianist, arranger, conductor, vocal coach, piano bar entertainer, orchestrator, and just about anything else that would pay me while I was trying to establish myself as a composer. I'd write songs for anything and anyone, and after a while I had quite a big pile of music written for various people and various projects. I met a wonderful young director named Daisy Prince, and she and I took this vast and unwieldy collection of material and began to shape it into a revue. By the time *Songs for a New World* opened at the WPA Theater in October 1995, we'd culled the sixteen songs that best suited our narrative purposes and our four exceptional singers. Four of those songs are included here. **"Stars and the Moon"** is without question my most popular and performed song, and I originally wrote it for a cabaret night at a summer stock theater in North Adams, Massachusetts; since its debut in 1991, its interpreters have included some of my favorite singers in the world, such as Karen Akers, Ann Hampton Callaway, Betty Buckley, and the magnificent Audra McDonald, who recorded it on her first album. **"I'm Not Afraid of Anything"** is the oldest song in this collection, having been written in 1990 for a cabaret night in Weston, Vermont. **"Just One Step,"** the story of a fed-up Upper East Side matron, was written specifically to showcase Laurie Beechman, who premiered it in Toronto. Finally, **"Hear My Song"** is the finale of the show, and it was originally written for Sally Mayes to sing at an AIDS benefit in New York. It's a song that gets done all the time at benefits and special events, and I'm very proud of this song's ability to inspire hope and strength within the performers and audiences who share it.

Parade is a musical based on the true story of the lynching of Leo Frank in Marietta, Georgia in 1915. The book for the show is by Alfred Uhry, and it was directed by theatrical legend Harold Prince. Alfred and I both won Tony Awards after the show's premiere at Lincoln Center Theater in 1998, and this score represents some of the most complex and ambitious writing I've done for the theater. **"The Old Red Hills of Home"** is the prologue to the show, sung by a young soldier as he prepares to join the Confederate Army and fight the Civil War. **"The Picture Show"** (published here for the first time) is a duet sung by young Mary Phagan and her prospective beau, Frankie Epps, as they ride on the streetcar the morning of the Confederate Memorial Day Parade. At the end of the controversial trial, Leo takes the stand and professes his innocence in **"It's Hard to Speak My Heart."** And on the eve of Leo's murder, he and his wife share a quiet jailhouse picnic, finally able to speak the words of their love to each other: **"All The Wasted Time."**

In 2002, Daisy Prince and I again collaborated on an Off-Broadway musical, *The Last Five Years,* a portrait of a doomed marriage between two young New Yorkers. I've chosen four songs from that show: **"See I'm Smiling"** is a scene in which Cathy, an actress, greets Jamie (her husband, an aspiring novelist) when he comes to visit the theater where she works. **"Moving Too Fast"** is a song I often use as an encore in my own concerts, in which Jamie expresses his astonishment that so many wonderful things are happening so quickly. **"A Summer in Ohio"** is Cathy's letter home to Jamie from her summer stock job. **"The Next Ten Minutes"** begins with Jamie's proposal to Cathy on the lake in Central Park, continues with the couple's wedding, and then ends by going backwards to Cathy's reaction to Jamie's proposal.

After *The Last Five Years* closed, I decided to take a break from writing full-scale musicals for a while so I could concentrate on my performing and songwriting, and the rest of this folio shows what I've been up to since then.

While she was starring in Trevor Nunn's production of *South Pacific* in London, Lauren Kennedy approached me about doing an album of my songs. When Lauren originated the role of Cathy in *The Last Five Years*, I thought she had one of the most powerful and expressive voices I'd ever heard, so we went through my trunk of songs and found a couple that took advantage of that amazing instrument, and then I wrote a whole bunch of new ones. The resultant album, *Songs of Jason Robert Brown,* introduced some of my more pop-oriented songwriting, and four of those songs are published here for the first time: **"And I Will Follow"** was originally written as part of a musical version of Oscar Wilde's story, "The Canterville Ghost," but when Lauren and I decided to use it, I rewrote most of the lyrics to fit as the opening of the album. **"Letting You Go"** and **"If I Told You Now"** were both written as stand-alone songs. **"Dreaming, Wide Awake"** was a song I wrote to explore a character that intrigued me, a young German girl who had helped found a group of Resistance fighters during World War II; I ultimately abandoned the project, but I'm very proud of this song and thankful to that young girl for her inspiration.

Two songs come from the Broadway musical **Urban Cowboy,** in which I led the onstage band and sang a number; the creative team asked if I would help with the score, and I was delighted to tailor several numbers to the talents of an incredibly gifted young cast. Bud, the hero of the show, sings **"It Don't Get Better Than This"** to explain why he came to Houston from a small town in West Texas. Sissy, a tough and sexy customer at Gilley's (the Houston music club in which the show takes place), shacks up with Bud until he accuses her of cheating on him – her furious response is **"Mr. Hopalong Heartbreak."**

And finally, in 2005, I released my first solo album, *Wearing Someone Else's Clothes,* a collection of songs I had written and recorded over the years that didn't fit into any of the shows I was writing. **"Someone to Fall Back On"** has served as the closing number for all of my concerts since I wrote it in 1998. **"Getting Out"** was written during a yearlong sojourn to Italy. **"I Could Be in Love with Someone Like You"** was actually the inspiration for *The Last Five Years*, and I'm thrilled to have this venue to put it out in the world. **"Nothing in Common"** was written as my toast at my brother's wedding. I wrote **"Grow Old with Me'** as part of the incidental music to David Lindsay-Abaire's magnificent play, *Kimberly Akimbo*. It seems most fitting to me to close the collection with **"Coming Together,"** a song I wrote in New York City during the devastating and confusing week after September 11, 2001.

And right now? After a long time in New York, I relocated to Los Angeles this year to teach at the University of Southern California and raise my beautiful baby daughter. In addition to touring the country performing, I'm in the middle of writing three new musicals, all of which will hopefully have been performed and shared with you all by the time my next collection rolls around in ten more years!

Jason Robert Brown
Los Angeles, California
January, 2006

contents

biography

JASON ROBERT BROWN has been hailed as "one of Broadway's smartest and most sophisticated songwriters since Stephen Sondheim" (*Philadelphia Inquirer*), and his "extraordinary, jubilant theater music" (*Chicago Tribune*) has been heard all over the world, whether in one of the hundreds of productions of his musicals every year or in his own incendiary live performances. *The New York Times* refers to Jason as "a leading member of a new generation of composers who embody high hopes for the American musical." Jason is the composer and lyricist of the musical, ***The Last Five Years***, which was cited as one of *Time Magazine's* 10 Best of 2001 and won Drama Desk Awards for Best Music and Best Lyrics. The original cast recording is available on Sh-K-Boom Records. Jason won a 1999 Tony Award for his score to ***Parade***, a musical written with Alfred Uhry and directed by Harold Prince, which premiered at Lincoln Center Theatre in December 1998, and subsequently won both the Drama Desk and New York Drama Critics' Circle Awards for Best New Musical. *Parade* was also presented on a national tour in 2000, which Jason conducted. Jason's first musical, ***Songs for a New World***, a theatrical song cycle directed by Daisy Prince, played Off-Broadway at the WPA Theatre in the fall of 1995, and has since been seen in more than two hundred productions around the world. Both shows were recorded for RCA Victor. Jason's scores are published by Hal Leonard Music. Jason is the winner of the 2002 Kleban Award for Outstanding Lyrics and the 1996 Gilman & Gonzalez-Falla Foundation Award for Musical Theatre. Jason's songs, including the cabaret standard "Stars and the Moon," have been performed and recorded by Audra McDonald, Betty Buckley, Karen Akers, Renée Fleming, Philip Quast, Jon Hendricks and many others.

Jason's first solo album, ***Wearing Someone Else's Clothes***, featuring his band The Caucasian Rhythm Kings, was released in June 2005 on Sh-K-Boom Records. His collaboration with singer Lauren Kennedy, ***Songs of Jason Robert Brown***, was released on PS Classics in April 2003. Jason is also the composer of the incidental music for David Lindsay-Abaire's *Kimberly Akimbo* and *Fuddy Meers*, Marsha Norman's *Last Dance*, David Marshall Grant's *Current Events*, Kenneth Lonergan's *The Waverly Gallery*, and the Irish Repertory Theater's production of *Long Day's Journey Into Night* and he was a Tony Award nominee for his contributions to the score of ***Urban Cowboy the Musical***. Jason's piano sonata, "Mr. Broadway" was commissioned and premiered by Anthony De Mare at Carnegie Hall, and he is writing a string quartet for Ethel, to be premiered in 2006. His next theater project, ***13***, a musical comedy written with Dan Elish, will premiere next season. Also in the wings: an musical adaptation of the 1992 film ***Honeymoon in Vegas***, in collaboration with screenwriter/director Andrew Bergman; and an as-yet-untitled new musical for Broadway with librettist Charlayne Woodard. Jason currently teaches musical theater performance and composition at the University of Southern California.

Jason studied composition at the Eastman School of Music in Rochester, N.Y., with Samuel Adler, Christopher Rouse, and Joseph Schwantner. He now divides his time between Los Angeles, California and Spoleto, Italy. Jason is a proud member of the Dramatist's Guild and the American Federation of Musicians Local 802.

jason robert brown

JUST ONE STEP
from *Songs for a New World*

Music and Lyrics by
Jason Robert Brown

"*Murray?*
I am out here, Murray. And I am not discussing this anymore!"

You don't wan-na buy me the fur? Well, that's just fine, Mur-ray. It's not like I'm ask-ing for much, since you won't buy me ___ the dog ___ Or the

8

15

What a sen-sa-tion-al fuck-ing ex-per-i-ence! Fin-al-ly, Mur-ray, I'm get-ting at-ten-tion! And

just one step! Look___ at where one step leads you: One small step

takes you___ high!___

Just one step___ down___ from the man who needs you! Fuck the

fur! Just send it down to her! So fare thee well, and

Mur - ray, Watch me Fly!

(Vamp until out of breath)

(Gasp!)

I'M NOT AFRAID OF ANYTHING

from *Songs for a New World*

Music and Lyrics by
Jason Robert Brown

Moderate Folk Rock

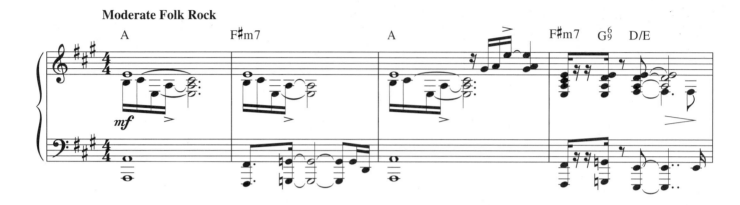

Jen-nie's a-fraid___ of wa-ter,___ I mean, she swims___ so well,___ but still, she's a-fraid of wa-

___ter.___ So she won't go near___ the sea...

D/E   F#m7sus

I'm not a - fraid_____ of an -

D6/9   A(add2)   E/G#

y-thing,_____ Be it moun - tains, wa - ter, drag - ons, dark____ or

F#m 9   D6/9

sky. I'm not a - fraid_____ of an -

F#m7sus/C#   D/B   A(add2)/C#

y-thing____ Tell me where's the chal - lenge if____ you nev - er try?

So let them call. And watch them fall.

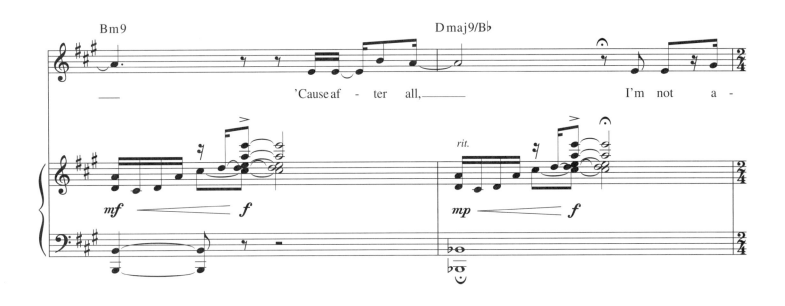

'Cause af - ter all, I'm not a -

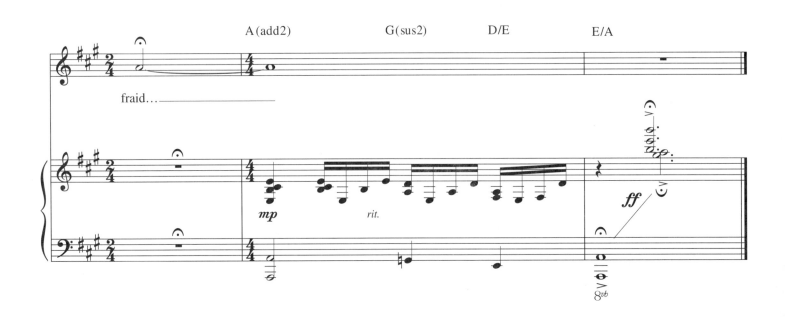

fraid...

STARS AND THE MOON

from *Songs for a New World*

Music and Lyrics by
Jason Robert Brown

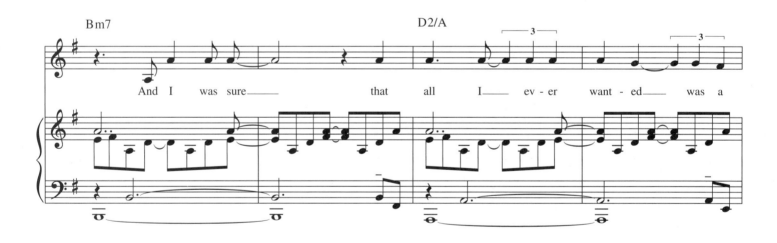

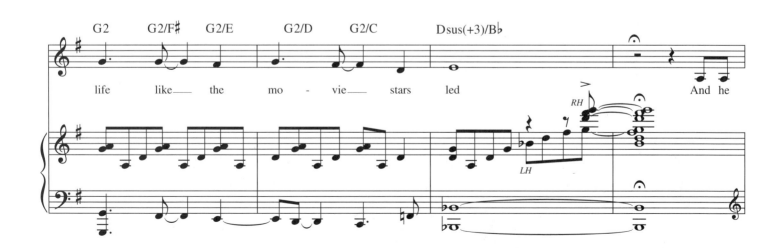

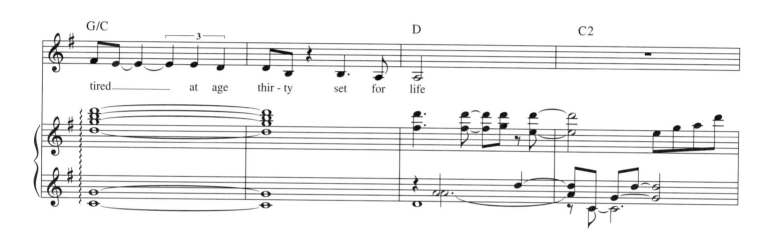

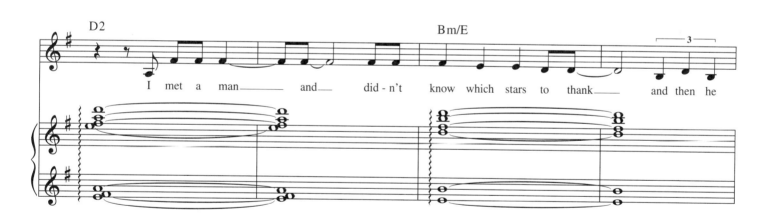

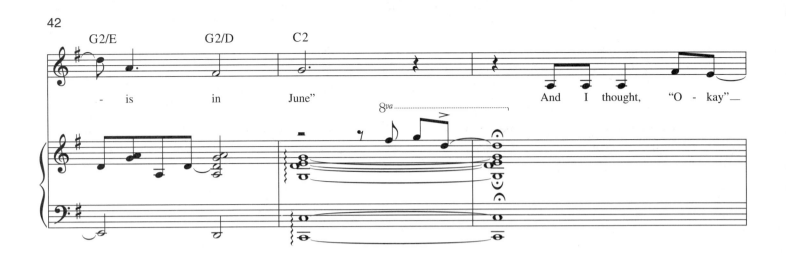

- is in June"   And I thought, "O - kay" —

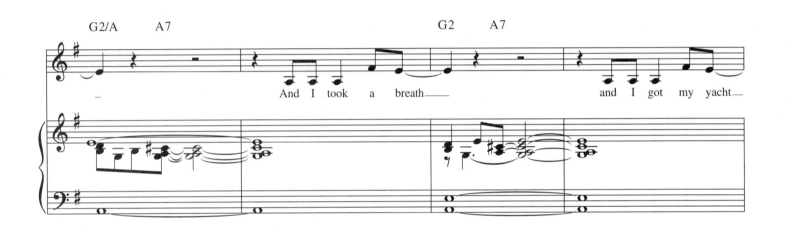

And I took a breath ___   and I got my yacht ___

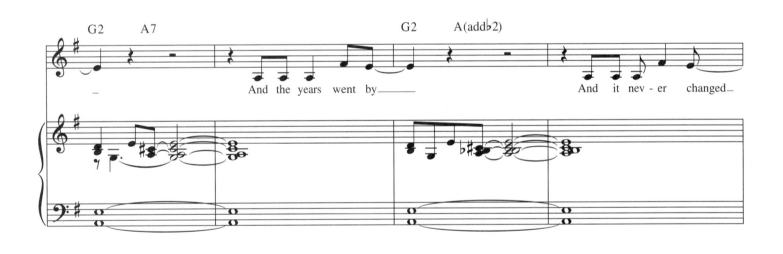

And the years went by ___   And it nev - er changed ___

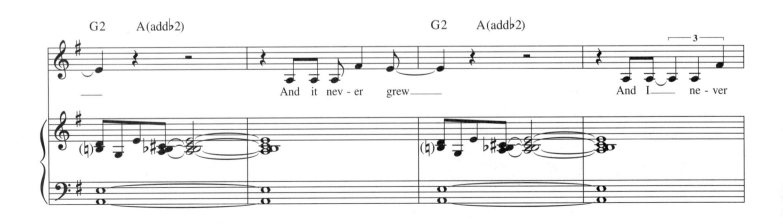

And it nev - er grew ___   And I ___ ne - ver

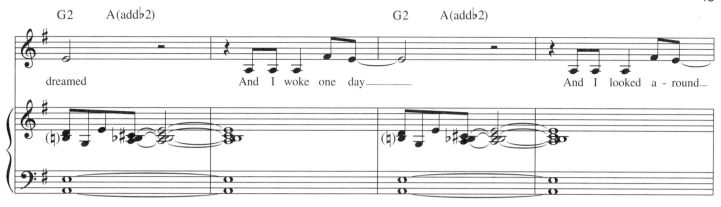

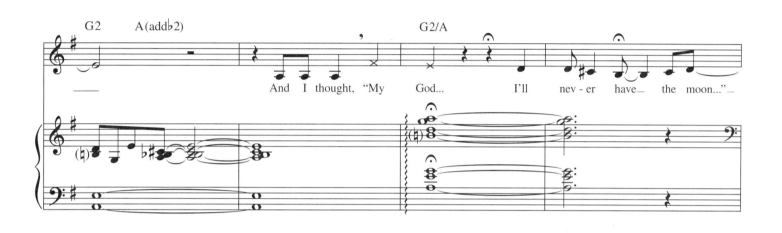

HEAR MY SONG

from *Songs for a New World*

Music and Lyrics by
Jason Robert Brown

Moderately, steady

Child, I know you're wear - y and your eyes want to close, and the days are get - ting long - er. We're not get-ting a-ny strong - er. Trust me, Ma-ma knows. But lie in my arms while you're sleep - ing, and

48

52

THE OLD RED HILLS OF HOME

from *Parade*

Music and Lyrics by
Jason Robert Brown

Steadily, with passion (= 88)

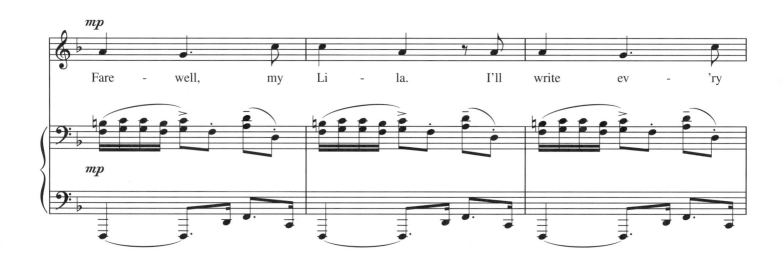

Fare - well, my Li - la. I'll write ev - 'ry eve - nin'. I've carved our___ names in the

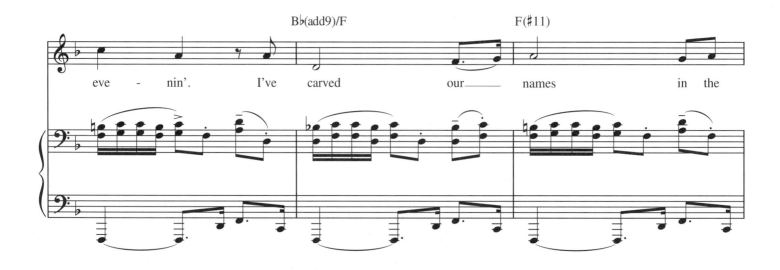

South - land _____ is free. _____

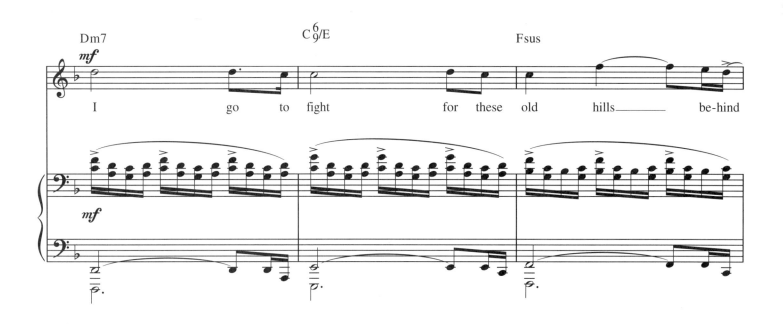

I go to fight for these old hills _____ be-hind

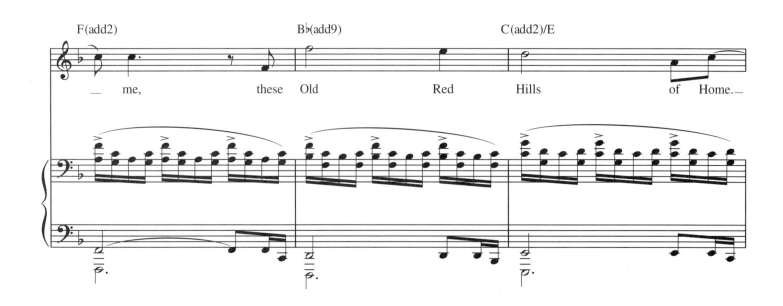

__ me, these Old Red Hills of Home. __

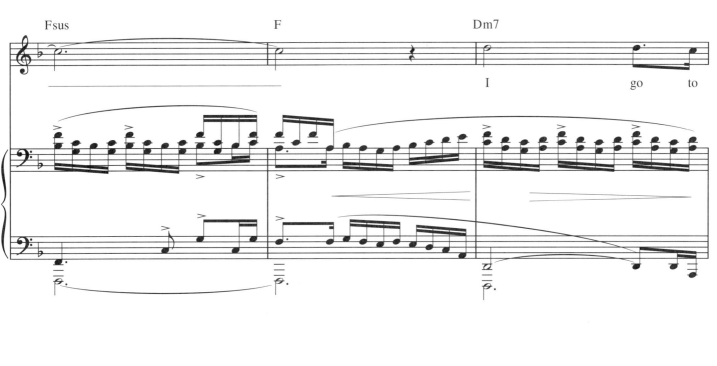

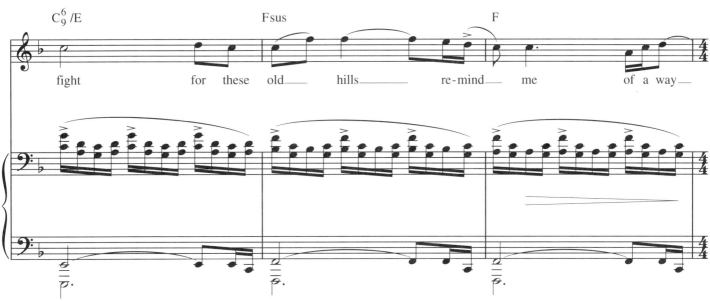

62

THE PICTURE SHOW
from *Parade*

Music and Lyrics by
Jason Robert Brown

Moderato, with a bounce (♩=104)

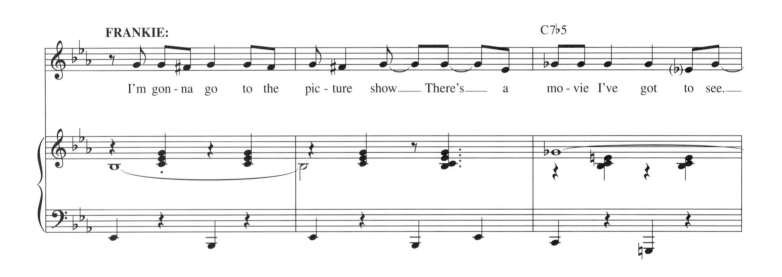

FRANKIE:

I'm gon-na go to the pic-ture show___ There's___ a mo-vie I've got to see.

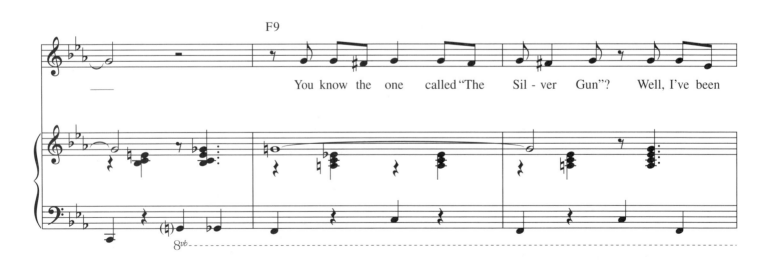

You know the one called "The Sil-ver Gun"? Well, I've been

FRANKIE: *Where you goin'?*
MARY: *To the factory. I didn't get my pay this week.*
FRANKIE: *Okay. I'll see you around.*

MARY: *At the picture show.*
FRANKIE: *What? I thought your Mama wouldn't let you!*
MARY: *She will with Essie and Betty Jean. Just not with you!*
FRANKIE: *Bye, Sunshine!*

De de,

de de, de de, de de, ska boo ba doo ba deet 'n dut 'n doo ba

doo doo doo. Go on, go on, go on, go on... **FRANKIE:** *Why, Iola! You goin' to the pictures tonight?*

IT'S HARD TO SPEAK MY HEART
from *Parade*

Music and Lyrics by
Jason Robert Brown

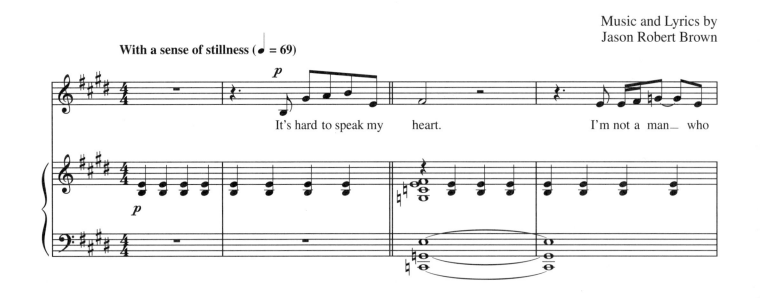

It's hard to speak my heart. I'm not a man who

bares his soul. I let the mo-ment pass me by; I stay where I am

in con-trol. I hide be-hind my work, safe and sure of what to say.

swear, I swore, we'd bare - ly met.

These peo - ple try to scare you

non cresc.

— with things I've nev - er said.

— I know it makes no sense. I swear I don't know

_mp_

Intensely

strongly

why… You see me as I am, You can't be-lieve I'd

f

lie. You can't be-lieve I'd do these deeds,

a lit-tle man who's scared and blind, too

mf

lost to find the words he needs.

ALL THE WASTED TIME

from *Parade*

Music and Lyrics by
Jason Robert Brown

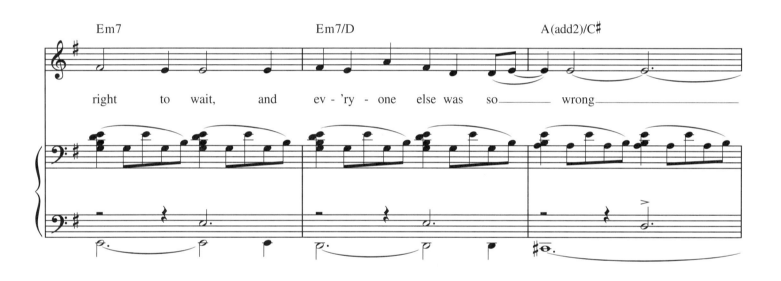

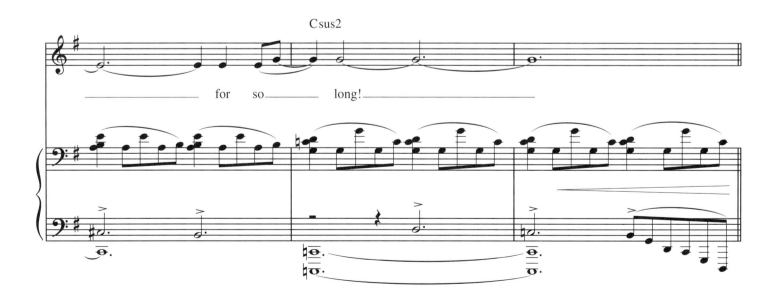

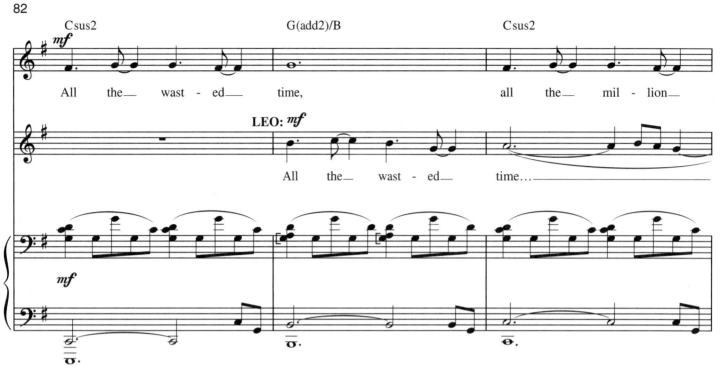

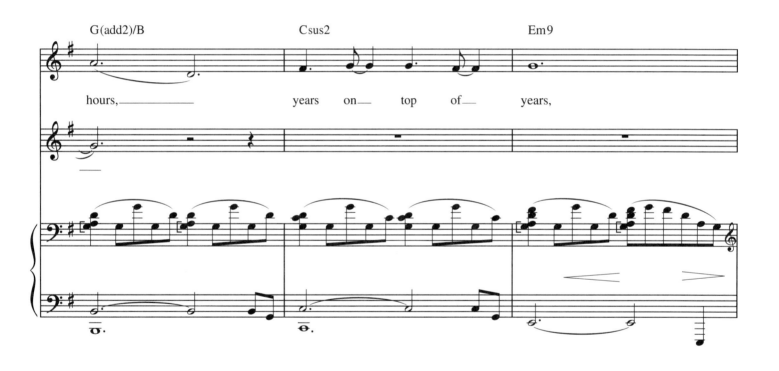

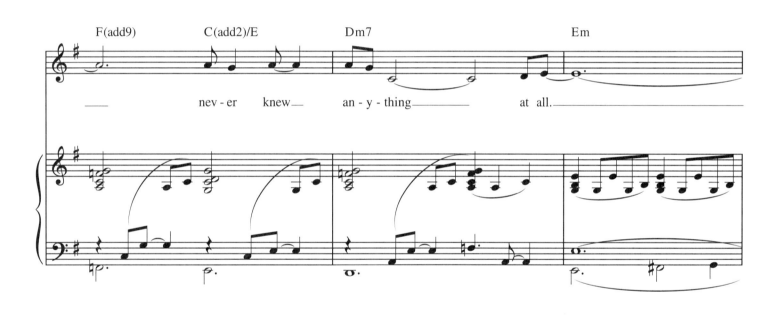

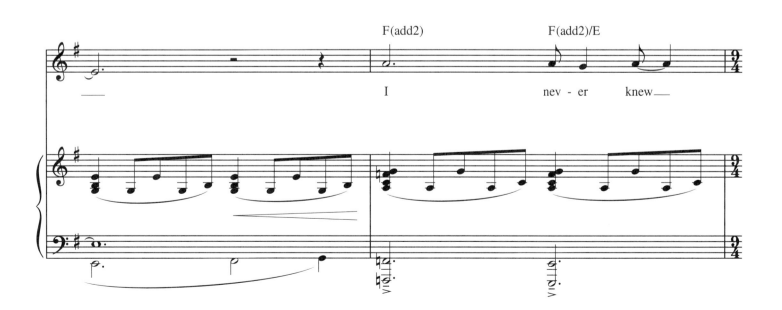

84

LEO: I nev - er knew— an - y - thing— at all!—

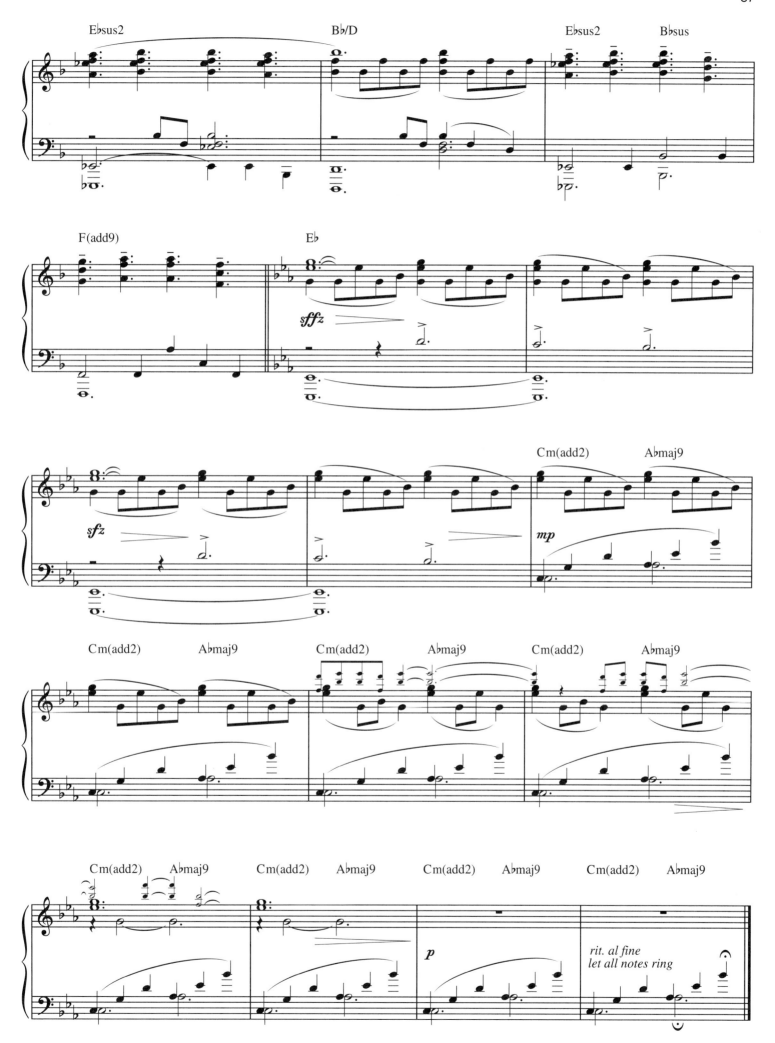

SEE I'M SMILING

from *The Last Five Years*

Music and Lyrics by
Jason Robert Brown

I guess I can't be-lieve_ you real-ly came_ And that we're sit-ting on_ this

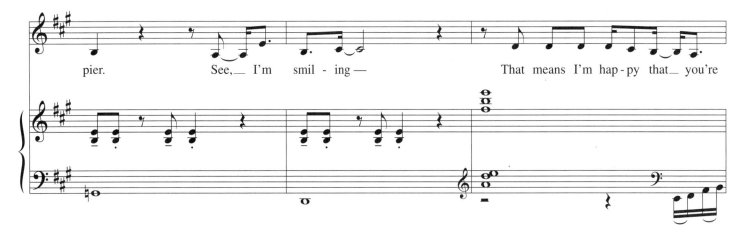

pier. See,_ I'm smil-ing — That means I'm hap-py that_ you're

here.

this love as spe-cial As it was___ five years___ a - go..

I mean, you made it to O - hi - o! Who knows_

where else___ we can go?___

I think you're real-ly gon-na like___ this show. I'm pret-ty sure_ it does-n't suck._

see what could be bet-ter — I'll own___ when I___ was wrong.. With all___ we've had___ to go___ through, We'll end___ up twice___ as strong. And so we'll start a - gain___ this week - end,___ And just___ keep___ roll - ing a - long...___

I did-n't know_ you had_ to go___ so soon... I thought we had a lit-tle time...

___ Look, what-e-ver,___ if you have to,___ Then you have to,___ so what-

e-ver.___ It's all right ——————————— We'll have to-night.

You know what makes me cra-zy? I'm sor-ry, can I say this? You know what makes me nuts? The fact that we could

be to-geth-er, Here__ to-geth-er, Shar-ing our night, spend-ing our time, And you are gon-na

choose some-one else to be__ with — no, you *are.* Yes, Ja-mie, that's ex-act-ly what you're do-ing: You could

be here with me, Or be there with them — As u-su-al, guess which you pick! No, Ja-mie, you do

MOVING TOO FAST

from *The Last Five Years*

Music and Lyrics by
Jason Robert Brown

Two thous-and bucks with-out__ re - writ-ing one word!

C7

Db7

I left Co - lum-bi - a and I don't re - gret it,

D7

I wrote a book and Son - ny Meh - ta_____ read it!

Eb7

E7

My heart's been sto - len! My_____ e - go's swol - len! I__

A SUMMER IN OHIO
from *The Last Five Years*

Music and Lyrics by
Jason Robert Brown

Moderate shuffle (♩=132-135)

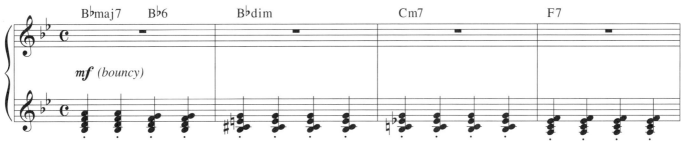

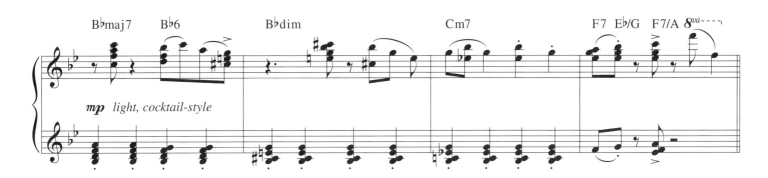

I could have a man-sion on a hill.__ I__ could lease a vil-la

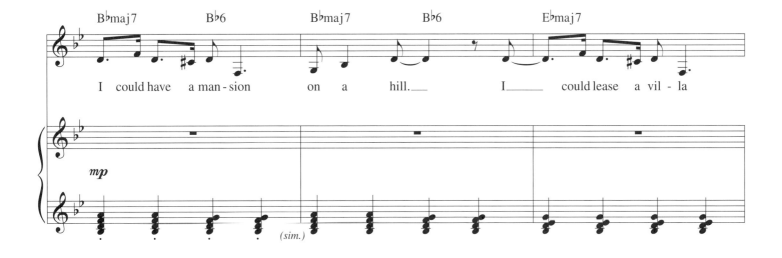

in Se-ville,__ But it would-n't be as nice_ As a sum-mer in__ O-hi-o With a

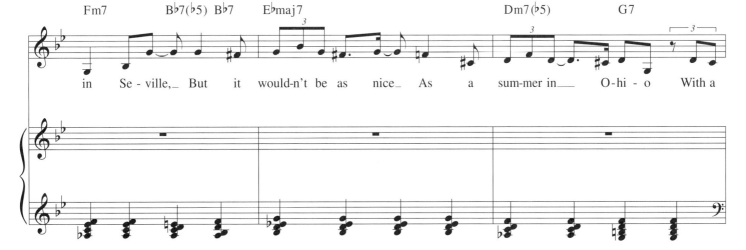

wants me, ___ he wants me, ___ But he ain't _____ gon-na get me! I've found my guid-ing light — ___ I tell ___ the stars ___ each night: Look at me! ___ Look at him! ___ Son - of - a - bitch! ___ I guess I'm do-ing some - thing _____ right! _____ I fin - 'ly ___ got ___

THE NEXT TEN MINUTES

from *The Last Five Years*

Music and Lyrics by
Jason Robert Brown

[*Ped.* throughout, change pedal on new harmonies]

IT DON'T GET BETTER THAN THIS

from *Urban Cowboy the Musical*

Music and Lyrics by
Jason Robert Brown

Moderato, in 2 (♩ = 88)

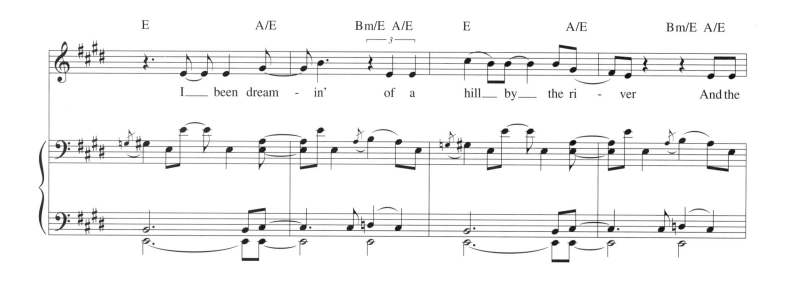

I_ been dream - in' of a hill_ by_ the ri - ver And the

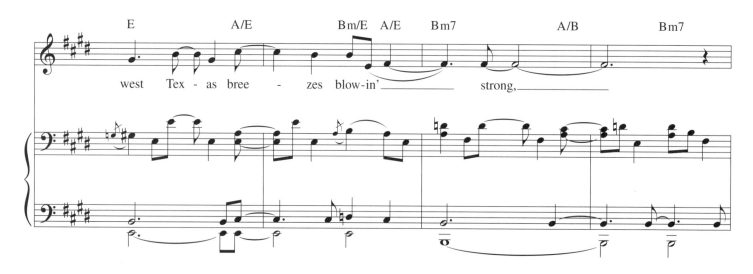

west Tex - as bree - zes blow - in'_____ strong,_____

130

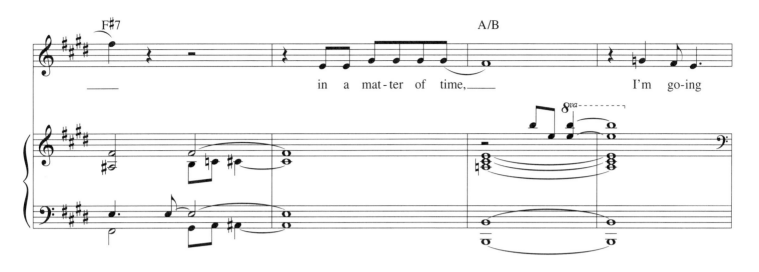

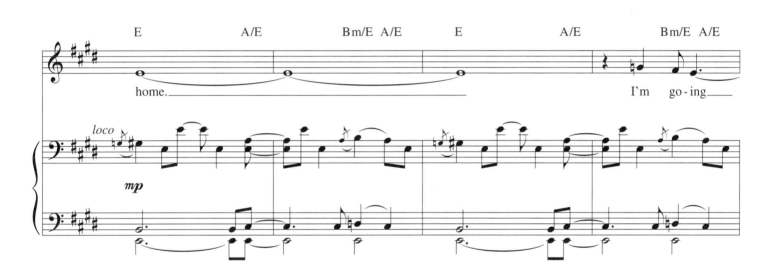

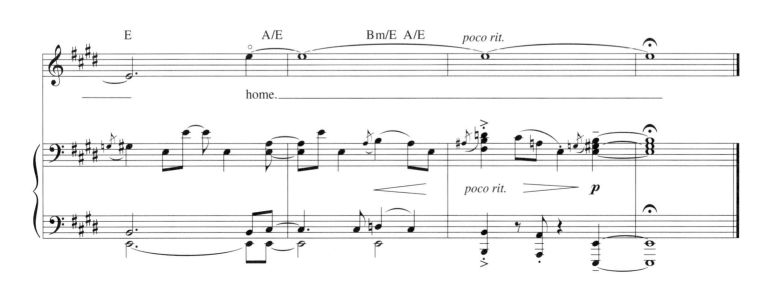

MR. HOPALONG HEARTBREAK
from *Urban Cowboy the Musical*

Music and Lyrics by
Jason Robert Brown

Bright Country Pop (♩ = 132)

So_ long, Fare - well, Mis-ter Hop-a-long Heart - break,_ Thanks for the kicks, but I

guess we're through. Oh_ well, it's been fun hitch-in' up with a psy - cho like

AND I WILL FOLLOW

Music and Lyrics by
Jason Robert Brown

Country Rock feel, with energy (♩.= 72)

Ask me_____ some-thing

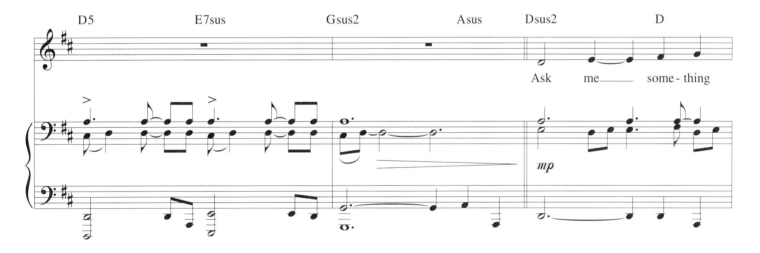

ea - si - er;_____ A smile, a kiss...

150

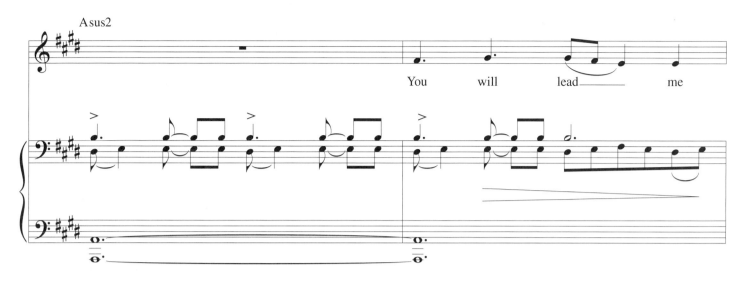

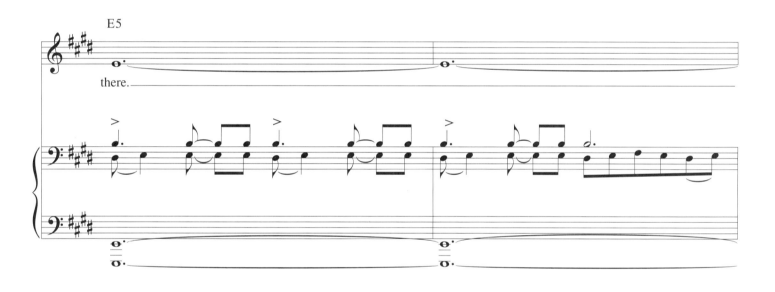

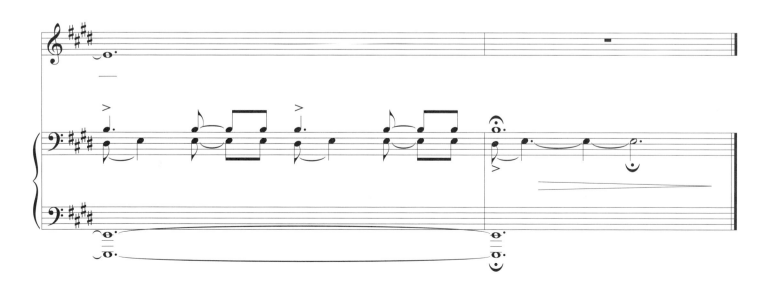

LETTING YOU GO

Music and Lyrics by
Jason Robert Brown

Slowly, thoughtfully

Sweep-ing up___ plas - ter,

Mop - ping___ the floor,___

Wash - ing___ the win - dows.

IF I TOLD YOU NOW

Music and Lyrics by
Jason Robert Brown

164

DREAMING, WIDE AWAKE

Music and Lyrics by
Jason Robert Brown

Flowing (♩· = 88)

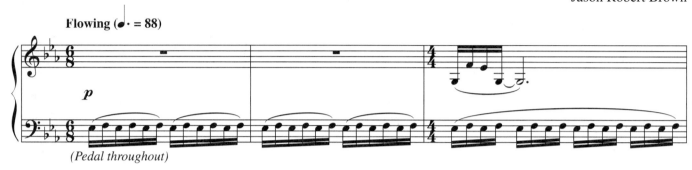

(Pedal throughout)

One of these days, I'll turn to wa - ter,

Fall from a cloud in - to the heat,

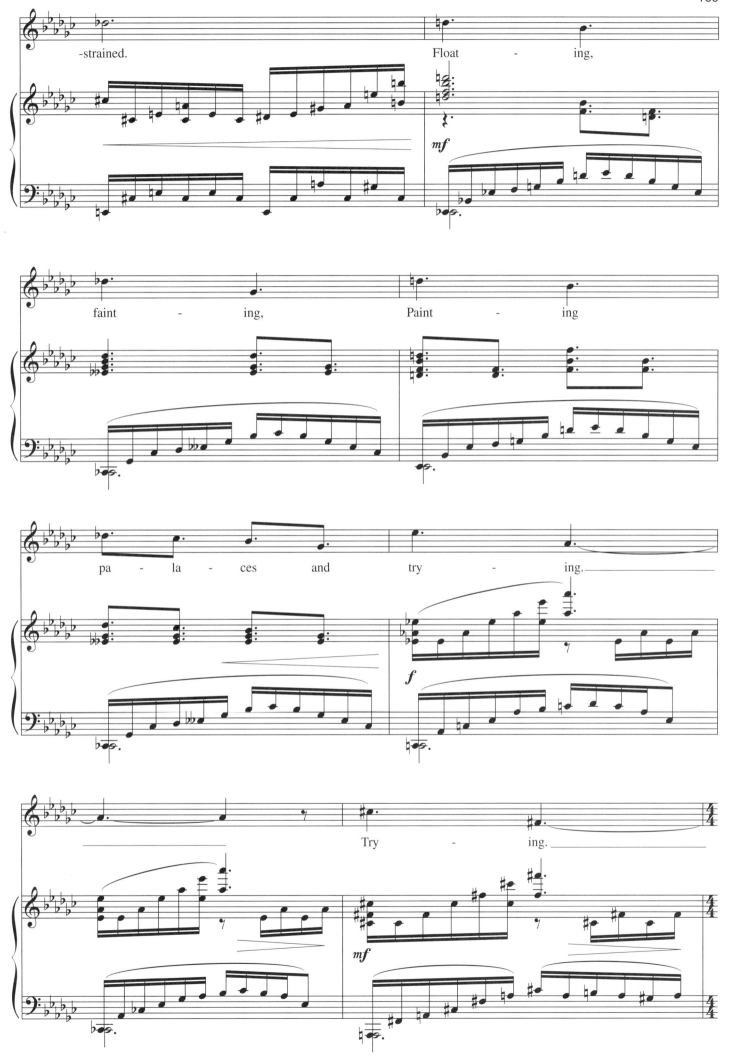

Watch how the wind is rush-ing through me.—

Look how the win-ter turns to spring.

If I can burst the clouds just breath - ing,—

Who knows what else my heart__ might____ bring?

Ev'-ry-one's scream - ing, scream - ing "Grow up!"__

Fun - ny, how I don't hear a

thing_____ For I'm

172

Burn - ing un - con - trolled, and

cry - ing.

Cry -

- ing!

Cry -

- ing!

This is how the eyes of the world are o - pened.

This is how the sun burns through the mist,

When

_mf_

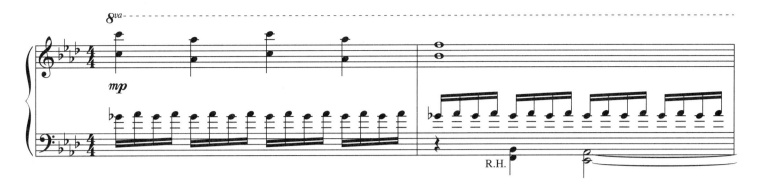

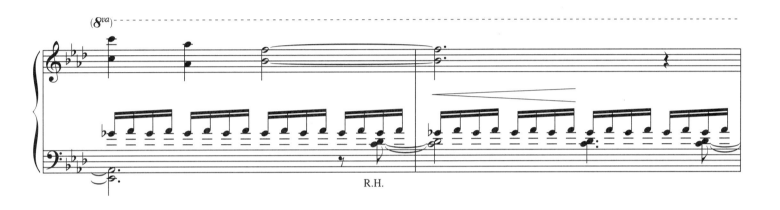

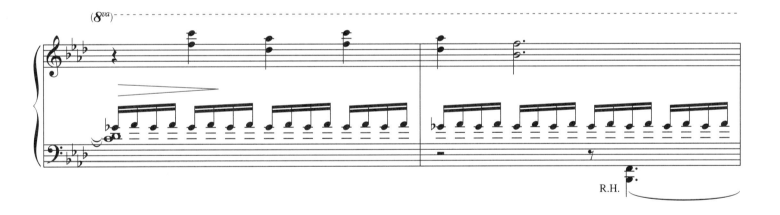

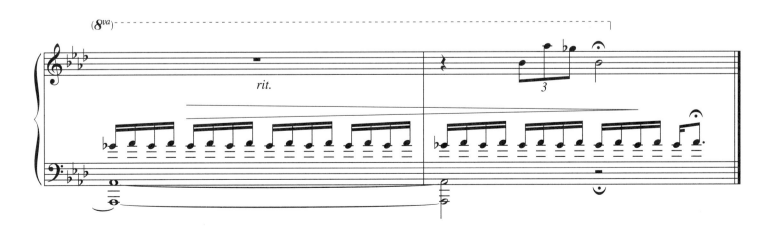

SOMEONE TO FALL BACK ON

Music and Lyrics by
Jason Robert Brown

Simply, with feeling (♩ = 80)

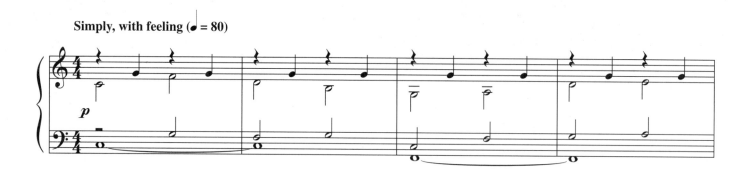

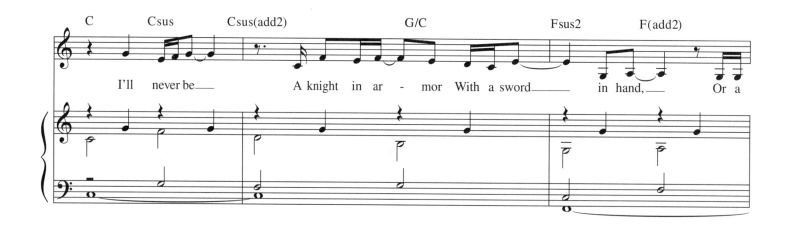

I'll never be___ A knight in ar - mor With a sword___ in hand,___ Or a

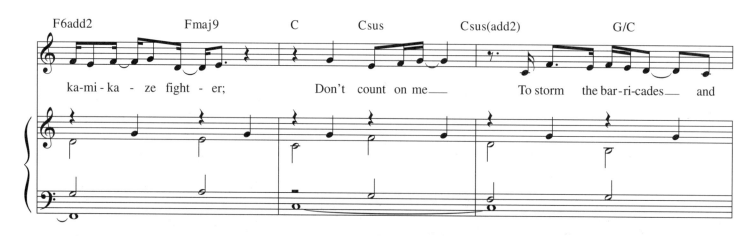

ka-mi-ka - ze fight - er; Don't count on me___ To storm the bar-ri-cades___ and

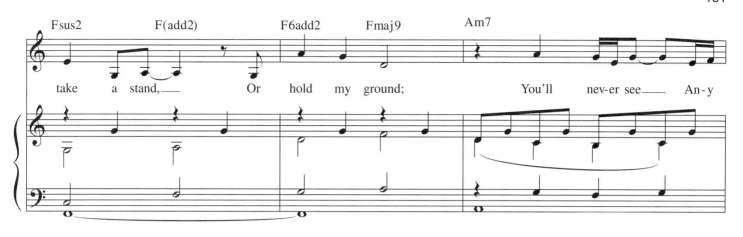

183

185

GETTING OUT

Music and Lyrics by
Jason Robert Brown

Hard Latino rock ($\half = 92$)

Mar-co plays pi - a - no. Mar-co's twen-ty - one.

189

191

Mar-co does a con - cert, Lines a-round the block.

Girls are there with their mid - riffs bare And the boys in a state of shock. They sell t -

- shirts and post-ers and au-to-graphed coast-ers; They're rak-ing in the bucks. With

GROW OLD WITH ME

Music and Lyrics by
Jason Robert Brown

Ring-a-ding swing

I COULD BE IN LOVE WITH SOMEONE LIKE YOU

Music and Lyrics by
Jason Robert Brown

208

212

NOTHING IN COMMON

Music and Lyrics by
Jason Robert Brown

There was this kid— A few— years back,— A lit - tle old - er than me,

Lived in my house and looked a lot— like my moth - er.—

218

223

COMING TOGETHER

Music and Lyrics by
Jason Robert Brown

Moderato, semplice

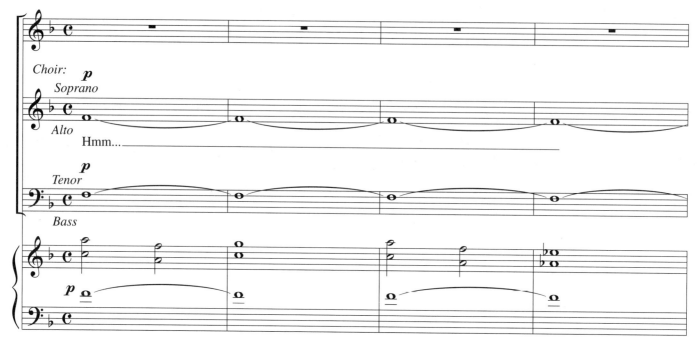

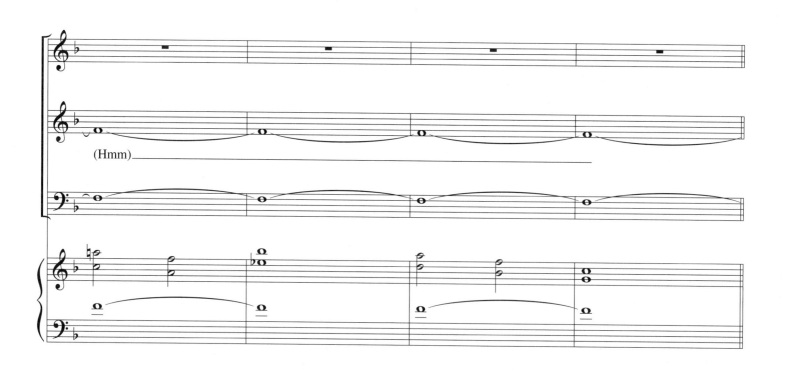

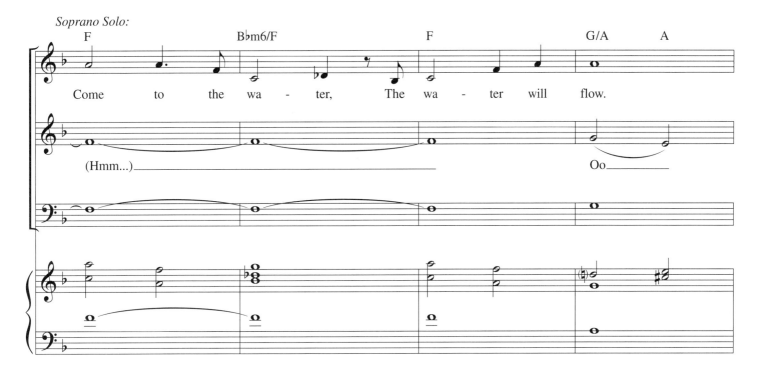

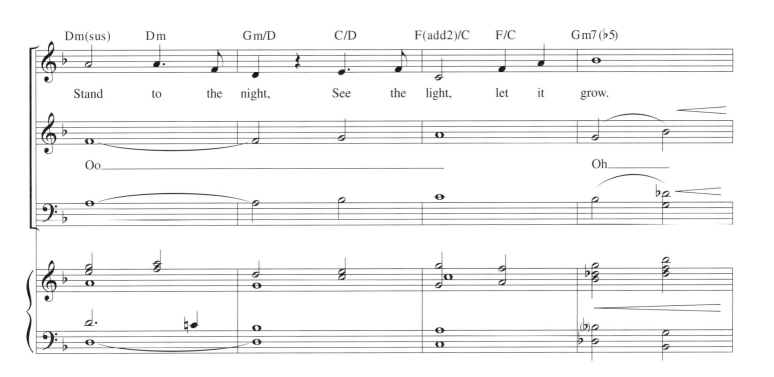

231

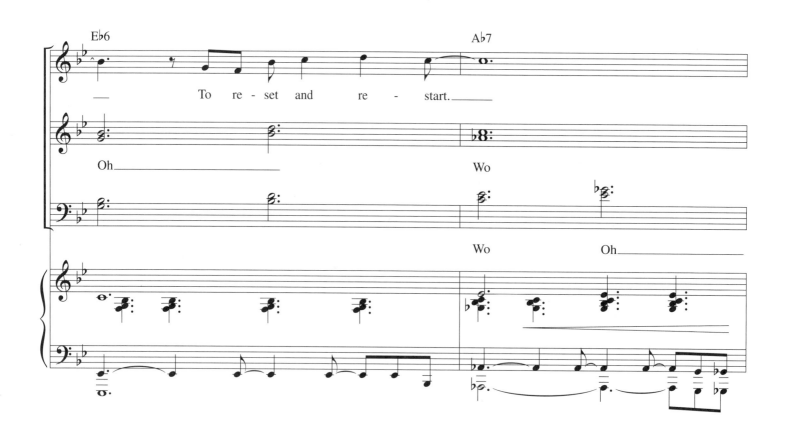

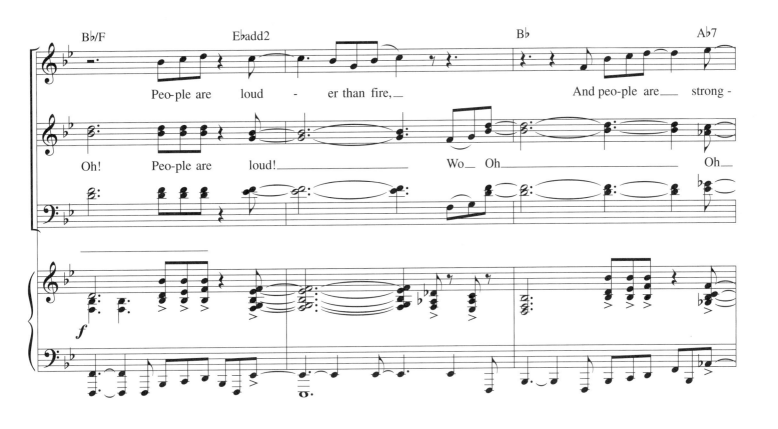

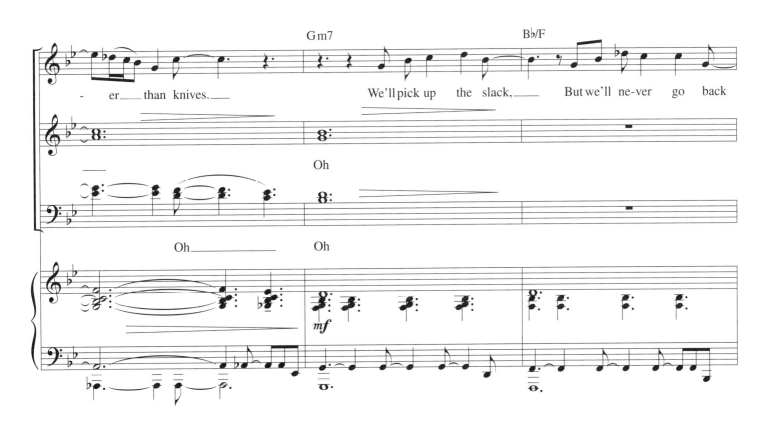

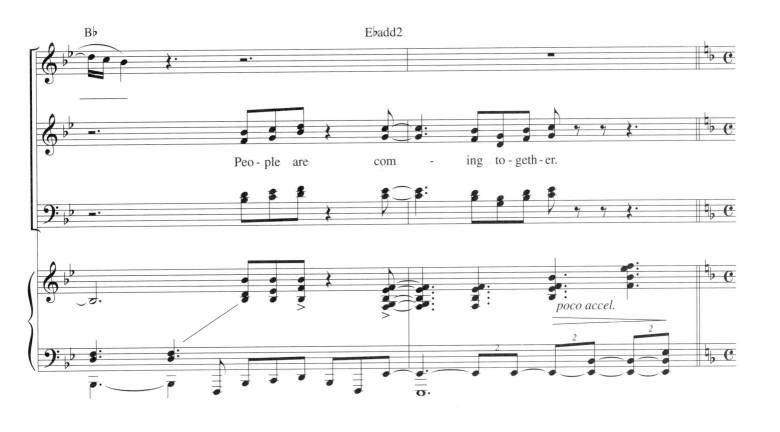

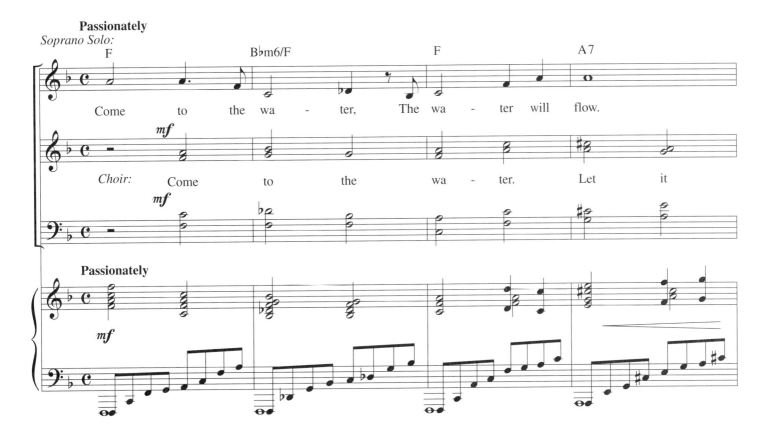

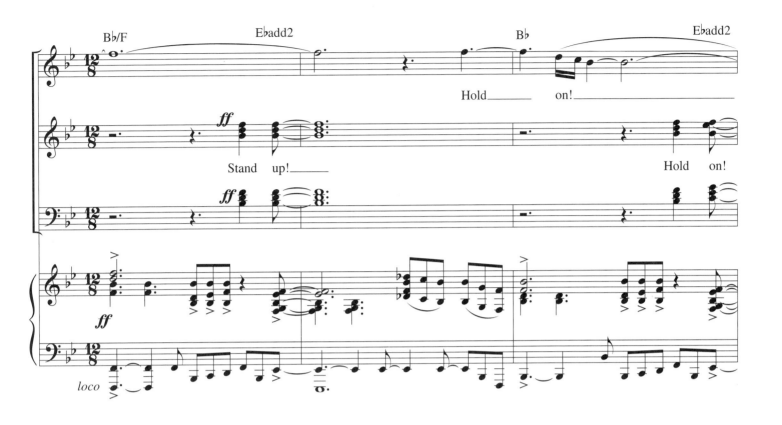

242

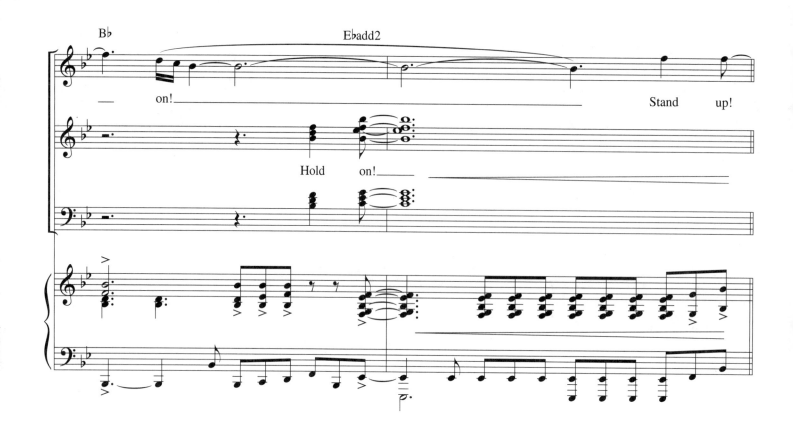

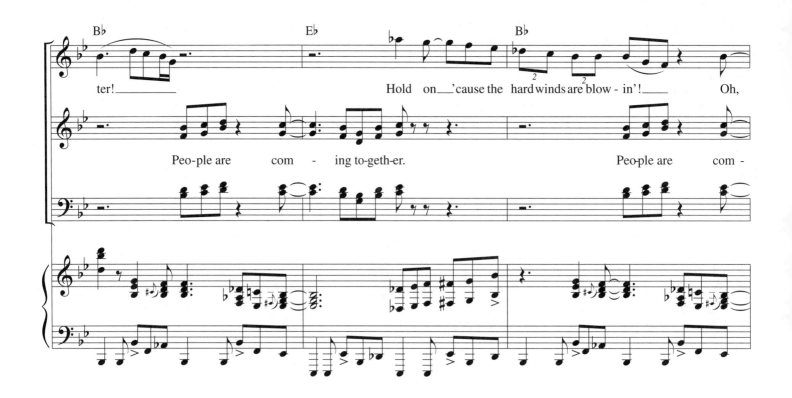

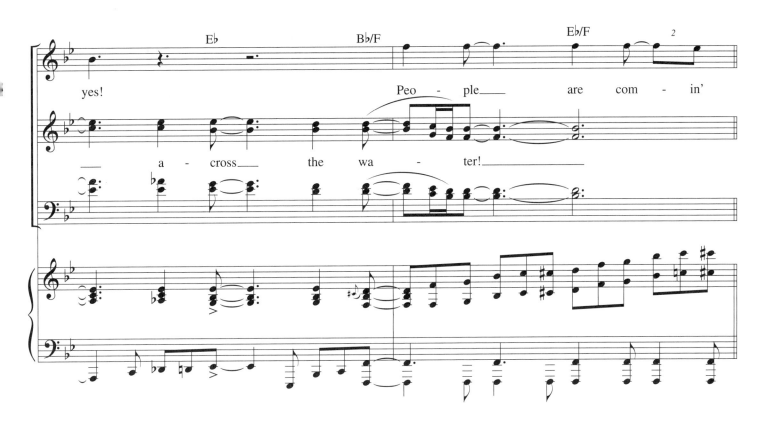

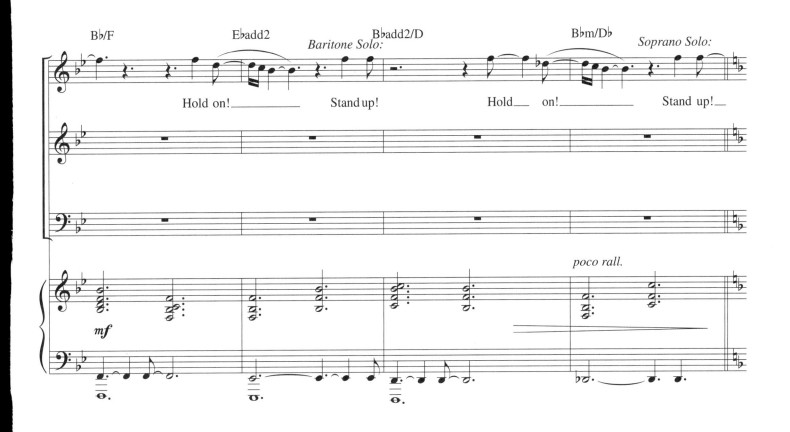

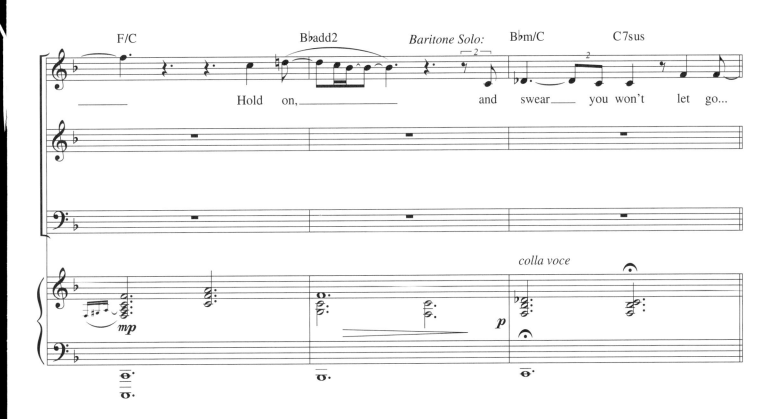

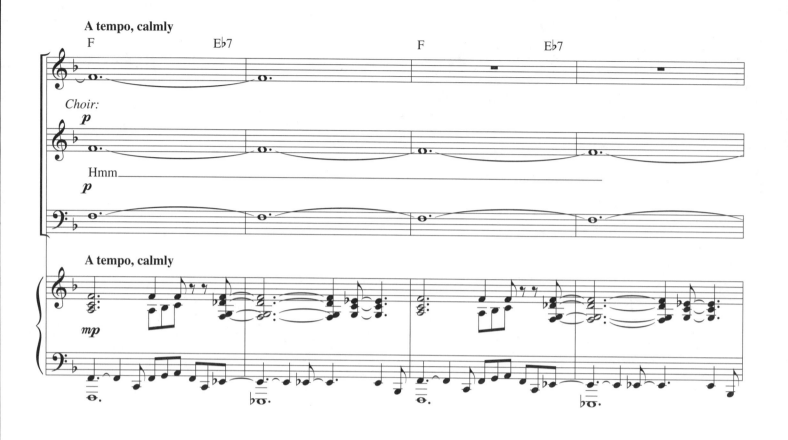

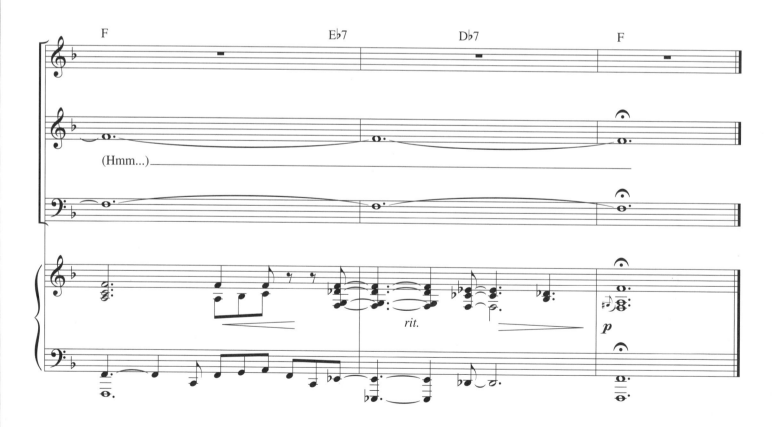